1997 Examination
Suggested Solutions

Evidence

LLB

University of London
External Examinations
Solutions by Michael Tookey
LLB, Barrister-at-law

HLT Publications

HLT PUBLICATIONS
200 Greyhound Road, London W14 9RY

Examination Questions © The University of London 1997
Solutions © The HLT Group Ltd 1998

All HLT publications enjoy copyright protection and the copyright belongs to The HLT Group Ltd.

All rights reserved. No part of this publication may be reproduced or transmitted in any form or by any means, electronic, mechanical, photocopying, recording or otherwise, or stored in any retrieval system of any nature without either the written permission of the copyright holder, application for which should be made to The HLT Group Ltd, or a licence permitting restricted copying in the United Kingdom issued by the Copyright Licensing Agency.

Any person who infringes the above in relation to this publication may be liable to criminal prosecution and civil claims for damages.

ISBN 0 7510 0835 4

British Library Cataloguing-in-Publication.

A CIP Catalogue record for this book is available from the British Library.

Printed and bound in Great Britain.

CONTENTS

Acknowledgement	iv
Introduction	v
Examination Paper	3
Suggested Solutions	
Question 1	11
Question 2	17
Question 3	23
Question 4	29
Question 5	35
Question 6	41
Question 7	47
Question 8	53

ACKNOWLEDGEMENT

The questions used are taken from the University of London LLB (External) Degree examination paper and our thanks are extended to the University of London for the kind permission which has been given to us to use and publish the questions.

Caveat

The answers given are not approved or sanctioned by the University of London and are entirely our responsibility.

They are not intended as 'Model Answers', but rather as Suggested Solutions.

The answers have two fundamental purposes, namely:

a) To provide a detailed example of a suggested solution to examination questions, and
b) To assist students with their research into the subject and to further their understanding and appreciation of the subject.

Note

Please note that the solutions in this book were written in the year of the examination. They were appropriate solutions at the time of preparation, but students must note that certain caselaw and statutes may subsequently have changed.

INTRODUCTION

Why choose HLT publications?

Holborn College has earned an international reputation for the outstanding quality of its teaching, Textbooks, Casebooks and Suggested Solutions to past examination papers.

Our expertise is reflected in the outstanding results achieved by our students in the examinations conducted by the University of London LLB Honours Degree Programme for External Students, the Council of Legal Education, and by students in over 70 universities who use our publications.

Suggested Solutions

The Suggested Solutions series provides examples of full answers to the problems posed by examiners. The solutions are much more than answers achievable by a candidate under examination conditions. The opportunity has been taken, where appropriate, to develop themes, suggest alternatives and set out additional material providing further comprehensive topical coverage.

To aid comprehension and revision, the solutions are fuller than would be possible under examination conditions. It is important to keep in mind that at this level there almost certainly is more than just one approach in answering any given question.

We feel that in writing full opinion answers we can assist you with your research and further your understanding and appreciation of the law.

Notes on examination technique

Although the SUBSTANCE and SLANT of the answer changes according to the subject-matter of the question, the examining body and syllabus concerned, the TECHNIQUE of answering examination questions does not change.

You will not pass an examination if you do not know the substance of a course. You may pass if you do not know how to go about answering a question although this is doubtful. To do well and to guarantee success, however, it is necessary to learn the technique of answering problems properly. The following is a guide to acquiring that technique.

Time

All examinations permit only a limited time for papers to be completed. All papers require you to answer a certain number of questions in that time, and the questions, with some exceptions carry equal marks.

It follows from this that you should never spend a disproportionate amount of time on any question. When you have used up the amount of time allowed for any one question STOP and go on to the next question after an abrupt conclusion, if necessary. If you feel that you are running out of time, then complete your answer in note form. A useful way of ensuring that you do not over-run is to write down on a piece of scrap paper the time at which you should be starting each part of the paper. This can be done in the few minutes before the examination begins and it will help you to calm any nerves you may have.

Reading the question

It will not be often that you will be able to answer every question on an examination paper. Inevitably, there will be some areas in which you feel better prepared than others. You will prefer to answer the questions which deal with those areas, but you will never know how good the questions are unless you read the whole examination paper.

You should spend at least 10 MINUTES at the beginning of the examination reading the questions. Preferably, you should read them more than once. As you go through each question, make a brief note on the examination paper of any relevant cases and/or statutes that occur to you even if you think you may not answer that question: you may well be grateful for this note towards the end of the examination when you are tired and your memory begins to fail.

Re-reading the answers

Ideally, you should allow time to re-read your answers. This is rarely a pleasant process, but will ensure that you do not make any silly mistakes such as leaving out a 'not' when the negative is vital.

The structure of the answer

Almost all examination problems raise more than one legal issue that you are required to deal with. Your answer should:

Identify the issues raised by the question
This is of crucial importance and gives shape to the whole answer. It indicates to the examiner that you appreciate what he is asking you about.

This is at least as important as actually answering the questions of law raised by that issue.

The issues should be identified in the first paragraph of the answer.

Deal with those issues one by one as they arise in the course of the problem
This, of course, is the substance of the answer and where study and revision pays off.

If the answer to an issue turns on a provision of a statute, CITE that provision briefly, but do not quote it from any statute you may be permitted to bring into the examination hall
Having cited the provision, show how it is relevant to the question.

If there is no statute, or the meaning of the statute has been interpreted by the courts, CITE the relevant cases
'Citing cases' does not mean writing down the name of every case that happens to deal with the general topic with which you are concerned and then detailing all the facts you can think of.

You should cite only the most relevant cases – there may perhaps only be one. No more facts should be stated than are absolutely essential to establish the relevance of the case. If there is a relevant case, but you cannot remember its name, it is sufficient to refer to it as 'one decided case'.

Whenever a statute or case is cited, the title of statute or the name of the case should be underlined
This makes the examiner's job much easier because he can see at a glance whether the relevant material has been dealt with, and it will make him more disposed in your favour.

Having dealt with the relevant issues, summarise your conclusions in such a way that you answer the question
A question will often say at the end simply 'Advise A', or B, or C, etc. The advice will usually turn on the individual answers to a number of issues. The point made here is that the final paragraph should pull those individual answers together and actually give the advice required. For example, it may begin something like: 'The effect of the answer to the issues raised by this question is that one's advice to A is that ...'

Related to the previous paragraph, make sure at the end that you have answered the question
For example, if the question says 'Advise A', make sure that is what your answer does. If you are required to advise more than one party, make sure that you have dealt with all the parties that you are required to and no more.

Some general points

You should always try to get the examiner on your side. One method has already been mentioned – the underlining of case names, etc. There are also other ways as well.

Always write as neatly as you can. This is more easily done with ink than with a ball-point.

Avoid the use of violently coloured ink, eg turquoise; this makes a paper difficult to read.

Space out your answers sensibly: leave a line between paragraphs. You can always get more paper. At the same time, try not to use so much paper that your answer book looks too formidable to mark. This is a question of personal judgment.

NEVER put in irrelevant material simply to show that you are clever. Irrelevance is not a virtue and time spent on it is time lost for other, relevant, answers.

EXAMINATION PAPER

UNIVERSITY OF LONDON
LLB EXAMINATIONS 1997
for External Students
PARTS I AND II EXAMINATIONS (Scheme A)
THIRD AND FOURTH YEAR EXAMINATIONS
(Scheme B)
GRADUATE ENTRY LEVEL II (Route A)
GRADUATE ENTRY THIRD YEAR EXAMINATIONS
(Route B)

LAW OF EVIDENCE

Thursday, 5 June: 10.00 am to 1.00 pm

Answer *FOUR* of the following EIGHT questions, including at least ONE from Part A and at least ONE from Part B.

PART A

1 Are there sufficient controls over the use of illegally obtained evidence other than confession evidence?

2 What are the main problems with identification evidence? Does the law of evidence deal with them adequately?

3 To what extent have recent similar fact cases clarified the law?

4 'It is the principle behind the right to silence, not its practical effect, which makes it necessary to reverse the recent reforms.'
   Discuss.

PART B

5 Andrew is charged with murdering Brian. The prosecution claimed that Andrew knifed Brian outside his house because he thought that Brian was having an affair with Carol, Andrew's wife. Andrew claims that he was defending himself because Brian attacked him when Andrew told him to 'put a stop to this nonsense with Carol'. A month before he died, Brian e-mailed his brother, saying he was scared because Andrew had found out about Carol and that he, Brian, would be 'looking over his shoulder from now on'. Doreen, Brian's sister, was staying at Brian's on the night of the

stabbing. She has stated to the police that she heard angry voices, amongst them Brian's voice, outside the house at the time. When the noise subsided, she went out to check and found Brian lying on the ground, bleeding, with no-one around. Brian said 'I tried to fend him off. He just went crazy.' Doreen says she won't testify because of anonymous telephone calls warning her against doing so. Sid, a detective who was pretending to be a prisoner at the time Andrew was in custody, says that he drew Andrew into a conversation in which Andrew said 'I gave Brian a right hiding. He had it coming to him all along.'

Discuss any evidential issues arising.

6 After a knife fight at a club, the police question everyone present. After this, and as a result, Ewan, Fred and George are arrested and charged with wounding with intent. During this initial questioning, Ewan makes a couple of admissions. The police search him at the police station, before his solicitor arrives, and they find that he has a number of pills. The police ask him what these are, and Ewan admits that they are 'a controlled drug'. Fred barely speaks English. The police hold him for nine hours while they obtain an interpreter. They then interview him and, in due course, he admits that he was involved in the fight. As a result of what Fred says, a bloody knife is found in a garden next door to the club. George is of very low intelligence, but the police are not aware of this, and George looks up to Ewan and Fred as his superiors. The police tell George that Ewan and Fred have admitted to being in the fight and, on hearing this, George admits that he himself took part and, further, played the major role. All three were offered access to a solicitor as soon as they reached the station, but only Ewan accepted the offer.

Discuss any evidential issues arising.

7 Half-Life Radiation plc, is collaborating with the Chemistry department of Faustus University. Together they are developing methods of producing chemical and radiated rain clouds for use by the Ministry of Defence. Particularly under investigation is the possibility of irradiating water with the use of small pellets of uranium. Harold, a lecturer in philosophy, who is investigating the moral status of such work, receives a massive overdose of radiation when he finds a batch of these pellets which have been carelessly left unprotected. He brings a negligence action against Half-Life Radiation plc, but the defendants refuse to disclose a report made by a special committee consisting of members of the Law and Chemistry departments of Faustus University. This committee had been created by the university after there had been a radiation leakage some years earlier. The terms of the Committee were 'to investigate the causes of accidents at Faustus'. Harold persuades his sister, Irene, who works for Half-Life Radiation plc, to give him a computer file of this report for him, saying that he needs it for his research. This file is clearly marked 'Confidential'. Harold finds that it

contains summaries of statements made by staff involved in the accident and the conclusions of the committee. Harold seeks to have this document admitted in evidence.

Advise Half-Life Radiation plc.

8 Joe and Kevin are charged with burglary of Lolita's house and Mervin is charged with handling a gold bracelet stolen in the burglary. Lolita testifies at trial that two men entered her bedroom one night. One, whom she identifies as Joe, held her down while the other, who was wearing a stocking over his face, ransacked her drawers. When they had gone, she called the police. Noel, a police officer, testifies that while driving to Lolita's house, he gave chase to two men who had acted suspiciously on seeing the police car. He stopped one, who was Kevin. Kevin had a stocking in his hand, and admitted the burglary. Noel also testifies that he found Lolita's bracelet when he later went to Mervin's jewellery shop. Joe testifies that on the night of the burglary he was in another town, attending Alcoholics Anonymous. He says he has 'never seen Mervin in his life'. Joe has two convictions, one for a bank robbery and another for taking ruby rings in a burglary. Kevin testifies that he tried to evade Noel because he'd 'had cops on him before'. Kevin says that when he was arrested he said [he] 'hadn't done anything', when accused of burglary. Kevin has been convicted for indecent assaults on young children and for tax evasion. Mervin testifies that he bought the bracelet from Joe, who had told him he was selling for his wife. In fact, Mervin had already told the police that he'd bought the bracelet from a 'man in the street'. Mervin's interview with the police is excluded by the trial judge because it contravened the Code of Practice.

Discuss the cross-examination of Joe, Kevin and Mervin.

SUGGESTED SOLUTIONS

QUESTION 1

Are there sufficient controls over the use of illegally obtained evidence other than confession evidence?

SUGGESTED SOLUTION TO QUESTION 1

General Comment

The modern case law on the judicial discretion to exclude relevant criminal evidence tends to obscure the fact that a very large number of cases every year involve arguments about the exclusion of non-confession evidence such as bodily samples, real evidence and evidence of acts by an accused which, although short of a confession, is evidence capable of supporting the case against him. Some discussion of the scope of ss78, 76(4), (5) and 82(3) Police and Criminal Evidence Act (PACE) 1984 and the common law discretion is called for.

Skeleton Solution

The main problems areas for non-confession evidence: bodily samples; unauthorised searches of persons or premises; evidence obtained by trickery or deception.
Control of the use of intimate samples.
Control of the use of real evidence obtained.
Control of the use of other evidence, including identifications.
Scope and relationship of the judicial discretions involved.
Conclusions.

Suggested Solution

The years since the enactment of PACE 1984 have seen a vast increase in the number and diversity of cases involving the judicial discretion to exclude relevant evidence in criminal trials. Because of the very wide meaning given to 'confession' by s82(1) and the common law, the large preponderance of cases dealing with confessions tends to obscure the importance of providing proper judicial control of other types of evidence. No less serious than confession evidence for an accused is the adducing by the prosecution of evidence of intimate bodily samples, items of real evidence or evidence of other activities by the accused, not consisting in a confession, which was, in each case, improperly or illegally obtained.

The question of the evidential use of intimate bodily samples is governed by ss62 and 65 PACE 1984. The most important point is that such samples may only be taken from a person in police detention by consent: s62(1)(b). Since the advent of DNA testing, the probative value of such evidence may be very high.

This will naturally increase the pressure to obtain such samples by improper means where consent is withheld, although scientific advances may allow for much greater significance and specificity to be given to non-intimate samples which are more easily obtained and can, in the circumstances set out in s63, be obtained without consent. The case of *R v Apicella* (1) shows that the Court of Appeal were unwilling to equate an intimate sample, taken in custody and without consent, with an oral confession; they upheld the judge's decision not to exclude it.

The problem with a decision such as *Apicella* is that it raises a temptation to abuse the opportunities for medical or dental treatment of a detained person, which occur as a routine matter, to obtain a non-consensual sample. It would be simplicity itself to obtain blood or month impressions from an emergency dental treatment. Although *Apicella* may have achieved a just result, it is hoped that the courts will do more than pay lip-service to the requirement for consent, in that it is a vital constitutional safeguard for detainees. *R v Nathaniel* (2) showed a much more principled approach to ss62 and 64(3B).

Many difficulties have arisen concerning evidence of substances or objects obtained as the result of unauthorised searches of premises or persons. There is clearly a tension involved here between the general admissibility of illegally obtained evidence, as explained by Crompton J in *R v Leatham* (3), and the protections given by Codes A and B of PACE 1984. The position of the accused is safeguarded only by the exclusionary discretions of the judge. The nature of these discretions is considered below but, if the test of 'fairness of the proceedings' (s78) is applied, it really does appear as if even quite serious breaches of the Codes will be overlooked by the courts provided that the means of obtaining the evidence does not, in itself, throw doubts upon its cogency. This much can be seen from cases such as *Jeffrey v Black* (4) (a pre-PACE 1984 case), *R v Stewart* (5) and *R v Wright* (6). This seems to confirm the pre-PACE 1984 distinction set out in *R v Sang* (7) between evidence obtained from a suspect after detention and other evidence concerning the discretion to exclude. Since PACE 1984 there is a discretion concerning such evidence which was not there at all before, according to *Sang*, but its exercise is fairly exceptional. This discretion is probably a sufficient control bearing in mind that 'fairness' means even-handedness to both sides.

Certain other types of non-confession evidence cause problems occasionally, such as identifications obtained in breach of Code D of PACE 1984, or tricking suspects into entering the jurisdiction from outside, where it is easier to obtain evidence against them (as in *R v Latif* (8)). Generally, this type of approach does not involve actual illegality by the police and the test of 'fairness of the proceedings' and the prejudice to the accused is a sensible yardstick to use; it seems reasonable to use a judicial exclusionary discretion where no illegality has been practised by the police. It can be argued that this should not be the case where the time-honoured recourse is had to the use of agents provocateurs to actually procure the commission of crime – but it is still English law that this will not provide a defence. It will be rare that the police will go so far into entrapment of persons as to become true agents provocateurs, in the sense used in *R v Sang*, but, as matters stand, evidence obtained by the police agents will continue to be admissible in law, subject only to the discretion to exclude according to *R v Smurthwaite and Gill* (9).

The principal judicial discretions in the above areas are the powers to exclude under ss78 and 82(3) which retain the common law discretions. It seems that the current judicial view is that s78 is at least as wide as the common law discretion as stated in *R v Sang* so, for present purposes, the paramount requirement is a fair balance between the two sides. Only time and the case law will determine whether this is a sufficiency of control in such a broad range of matters, but it seems that the courts are maintaining their consistent approach of general admissibility of evidence regardless of dubious methods of acquisition. This is allied to an exclusionary discretion of great width but which must be governed by balancing the interests of the parties. The House of Lords examined the scope of s78, the common law discretion and art 8 of the European Convention and their interrelationship in *R v Khan (Sultan)* (10).

References

(1) (1985) 82 Cr App R 295
(2) [1995] 2 Cr App R 565
(3) (1861) 8 Cox CC 498
(4) [1978] QB 490
(5) [1995] Crim LR 500
(6) [1994] Crim LR 55
(7) [1980] AC 402
(8) [1996] 1 All ER 353
(9) [1994] 1 All ER 898
(10) [1996] 3 WLR 162

QUESTION 2

What are the main problems with identification evidence? Does the law of evidence deal with them adequately?

SUGGESTED SOLUTION QUESTION 2

General Comment

This type of question calls for a fairly analytical view of the legal rationales and mechanisms involved in placing identification evidence before the court. Some discussion of the underlying problems of this type of evidence and the basic safeguards provided by *Turnbull* is called for, as well as discussion of the hearsay problem involved in providing evidence of out of court identifications by witnesses other than the identifying person. Some reference to identification by descriptions, sketches, photofits, photographs and the like should be made.

Skeleton Solution

The underlying problem of unreliability of eyewitness identification; the genesis of the *Turnbull* guidelines.

The *Turnbull* guidelines and subsequent applications.

Adducing identification evidence; the difficulties for the eyewitness and witnesses of the act of identification.

Dock identification.

The evidential use of descriptions and representative images.

The evidential use of photographic images.

The application of *Turnbull* to descriptions, images and photographs.

Suggested Solution

One of the most terrible possibilities in the use of evidence is that of a conviction based upon mistaken eyewitness identification. The nature of many offences is that witnesses see the perpetrator briefly or under bad conditions of visibility or both. Widespread dissatisfaction with the situation after a series of high-profile cases led to the matter being investigated by the Criminal Law Revision Committee and by a special committee chaired by Lord Devlin, which went so far as to recommend changing the law so as to prevent convictions based substantially on eyewitness identifications. Within a very short period, the Court of Appeal under Lord Widgery CJ had the opportunity to hear conjoined appeals in several eyewitness identification cases, and the court set out a series of guidelines to clarify matters which have become known as the *Turnbull* guidelines after *R v Turnbull* (1).

The guidelines, which have proved practicable in application, do not follow the recommendation against allowing convictions relying substantially on identification evidence but, instead, impose positive and detailed requirements upon the trial judge as to his handling of the case and his directions to the jury. The essence of the guidelines is that, in cases where the identification evidence is central to the Crown's case, the judge must warn the jury of the special need for caution in convicting on such evidence and of the special dangers inherent in this type of evidence and witness, the ease of making mistakes and the dangerously convincing nature of the evidence. He must positively draw attention to weaknesses and inconsistencies in the evidence, including: the conditions of light and observation, range and duration etc, as in *Turnbull* itself; weaknesses and inconsistencies in the evidence whether picked out by the defence or not (*R v Fergus* (2)); and inconsistencies between the identifying witnesses (*R v Barnes* (3)). Evidence of recognition should be specifically dealt with, and the possibility of mistake alluded to, except in circumstances where there is no possibility of mistake: *Beckford v R* (4). After different views earlier, the view of the Privy Council seems to be that even where fabrication and lies by the witnesses are alleged, a *Turnbull* warning should be given to identification or recognition evidence: *Beckford v R; Shand v R* (5).

The judge must assess the quality of the identification evidence, according to *Turnbull*. If it is (by at least one witness) of good quality, he may then leave it to the jury along with his warning. If, by contrast, it is of poor quality unless there is other evidence (perhaps identification of another suspect who was associated with the accused as in *R v Penny* (6)) which is capable of supporting the identification, he should withdraw the case from the jury and direct an acquittal. Generally, the guidelines seem to have functioned very well and have not really required modification. To this extent, they seem to have justified the confidence in identification evidence shown by Lord Widgery CJ, and to have overcome most of the dangers of mistaken identity leading to conviction.

Some difficulties have arisen over the years in situations where the identifying witness is dead or unable to remember the identification or for some other reason there is a need to produce another witness, such as a police identification officer, to give evidence that the accused was actually identified by the eyewitness out of court. The obvious problem is that such evidence, conceptually, has a hearsay component. The courts seem to have adopted a fairly pragmatic view of this situation, at least so far as formal identification proceedings are concerned. It may be the view that the identification officer is giving his own, direct original testimony of what he himself perceived or it may be, as Lawton LJ said in *R v Osbourne, R v Virtue* (7), that as identification parades are authorised by statute and are, generally, for the protection of the accused, evidence of the parade should not be hindered by 'artificial rules of evidence'. It is difficult to know whether the old rule in *R v Gibson* (8) against allowing in informal identifications out of court would still apply; possibly it would as these are nowhere contemplated by statute.

There are undoubtly problems of prejudice in permitting, for the first time, a dock identification (other than recognition). In a situation where any of the

Code D methods have been available, a dock identification should not generally be permitted (*R v John* (9)), but this question does seem to be a matter within the discretion of the court according to the Court of Appeal in *North Yorkshire Trading Standards Dept v Williams* (10). Considering the difficulties attending identification, this is a sufficient safeguard, bearing in mind the general rule of discretion to exclude exceptionally prejudicial evidence at common law.

Sometimes, the witness cannot identify a person but has either by his own hand, through the agency of others or of equipment, produced a description or image against which the accused is to be judged. A description is the witness's own perception and he can usually give direct testimony of the matter. Other generated images were considered by the Court of Appeal in *R v Cook* (11) to be sui generis and outside the rules against hearsay or narrative.

Occasionally, the only witness to an offence is a camera recording either still or moving film from which a suspect has been identified. The film itself is real evidence and, as such, prima facie admissible (*R v Dodson* (12)), but the real purpose in admitting the evidence is to identify the accused and this decision is one for the jury. The real problem with descriptions, images and photographs is whether they should be subject to the *Turnbull* guidelines. In *R v Constantinou* (13) it was held that a photofit created from descriptions did not need a *Turnbull* warning. This sounds very risky as there is no difference, in principle, between identification and description. This decision seems to be inconsistent with the earlier, more logical proposition in *Taylor v Chief Constable of Cheshire* (14) which supports the view that a *Turnbull* warning ought to apply (in an identification from security camera situation) to the position of the camera and the locus of the crime, the reproduction tape and viewer and the position of the 'identifying witness' (ie often the jury itself). It is submitted that a *Turnbull* warning should, for safety's sake, be given whenever an accused is sought to be identified from evidence or a source involving eyesight.

References

(1) [1977] QB 224
(2) (1994) 98 Cr App R 313
(3) [1995] 2 Cr App R 491
(4) (1993) 97 Cr App R 409
(5) [1996] 1 All ER 511
(6) (1992) 94 Cr App R 345
(7) [1973] 1 QB 678
(8) (1887) 18 QBD 537
(9) [1973] Crim LR 113
(10) (1994) The Times 22 November
(11) [1987] QB 417
(12) (1984) 79 Cr App R 220
(13) (1990) 91 Cr App R 74
(14) [1987] 1 All ER 225

QUESTION 3

To what extent have recent similar fact cases clarified the law?

SUGGESTED SOLUTION TO QUESTION 3

General Comment

Few areas of common law have seen such diversity of views among the higher appellate judges as the development of the similar fact evidence doctrine. The recent judgments in the House of Lords have achieved a clarity of sorts, but they may, paradoxically, have created greater difficulties for those least able to cope with the complexities involved, the jurors. There should be some limited exposition of the pre- and post-*Boardman* law, a review of the important House of Lords decisions since *R v P*, and some attempt at a firm conclusion about clarification one way or the other (either view is quite supportable).

Skeleton Solution

Development of the similar fact evidence doctrine: *Makin; Boardman;* application of *Boardman*.

R v P – significance of the judgment.

R v H – significance of the judgment.

Other cases since *R v P*.

Cumulative effect of recent cases.

Conclusion.

Suggested Solution

Very few other areas of the law of evidence have exercised the minds of the appellate judges to the extent of cases concerning similar fact evidence. This type of evidence, inevitably highly prejudicial, is always seen as being in tension with the judicial discretion to exclude evidence, the prejudicial effect of which outweighs its probative value. The nature of such evidence is that, once admitted, it usually convicts. Such is the caution that courts have exercised with similar fact evidence that very lengthy judicial analysis has been given to it on a frequent basis over, at least, the last century or so. Similar fact evidence may be described as evidence indicating a disposition to act in a certain way on occasions other than the circumstance for which a person is being tried. Such evidence, normally inadmissible, as dangerously prejudicial but irrelevant, is admissible, by way of exception, where it has true relevance to the instant charge. The relevance can be shown in an infinite variety of ways, but relevance or probative value (which is the same thing) there must be, sufficient to outweigh prejudice.

The origins of the modern view can be seen in Lord Herschell's seminal speech in *Makin v Attorney-General for New South Wales* (1) which formulated the general rule of exclusion of similar fact evidence and went on to postulate a general exception allowing admissibility on the basis of relevance to the issues in the case. He perhaps unfortunately, went on to give examples of such relevance, such as rebutting defences fairly open or questions of accident. The tendency after *Makin* was to try to bring evidence within various categories of exception which, so it was argued, were expressly or impliedly admissible by Lord Herschell's speech. The problem was that the cases subsequent to *Makin* developed ever more technical distinctions, often based upon the defences relied upon or the explanations given by the accused as a rationale for admissibility. This rationale of relevance based upon defences fairly available, as distinct from defences actually relied upon, means that similar fact evidence can be led in evidence-in-chief by the prosecution: *Harris v DPP* (2).

The doctrine received a good deal of consideration and some very welcome clarification in *DPP v Boardman* (3). The main benefit of the judgments in *Boardman* is the general disavowal of a principle of admissibility based upon established categories of situation. The only real principle justifying admissibility of such dangerously prejudicial evidence is probative value; in *Boardman*'s case, arising from the 'striking similarity' of the different witness accounts. Such probative value may arise, not from striking similarity at all, but from something as mundane as the unlikelihood of coincidence in the stories told by completely unconnected witnesses. The judges in *Boardman* do seem to rely quite heavily on the inexplicability of such evidence on grounds of coincidence. The problem with *Boardman* is that it does tend to emphasise the 'striking similarity' or 'special feature' rationale and to obscure the fact that probative force can come from other directions. One of the difficulties that arose in cases over the next few years was the unwillingness to admit into evidence behaviour which was said to be 'no more than the stock-in trade' of certain types of offender (as in *R v Inder* (4) and *R v Novac* (5)) and, indeed, in the Court of Appeal in *R v P* (6).

A considerable shift of emphasis could be seen when *R v P* was decided by the House of Lords. Dealing with the particular situation of the cross-admissibility of the evidence of the alleged two victims of incest, it being devoid of unusual features (beyond the incest itself), the House of Lords stated, as a general principle, that in cases where there was no issue as to identity of the offender, there was no requirement to look for special features or 'striking similarity'. This is quite a monumental change, and all that needs to be looked for is 'probative force'. This has been used to link offences of robbery in *R v Laidman and Agnew* (7) without any special features at all, and seems to have been extended, with frightening effect, to the possession of quite small sums of money (£135) as evidence of drug dealing, along with a mobile phone and some plastic bags as evidence of the paraphernalia of drug dealing, in *R v Wilkinson, R v Fraser* (8), although the Court of Appeal indicated that to admit such a small cash sum into evidence was 'at the limit' of the judge's discretion.

A further considerable change of thinking came about as illustrated in *R v H* (9), where the House of Lords departed from earlier views by holding that the similar fact evidence from two alleged victims of sexual offences where there was, at least, a risk of collusion, should be admitted on the assumption that the witnesses are truthful and the question of collusion be left to the jury as going to weight rather than admissibility. This is absolutely contrary to the earlier position which would generally have kept the evidence out because of the dangers of such evidence.

Other recent cases have shown a greater willingness to treat similar fact evidence as being something that juries can deal with in a relatively structured and analytical way. In *R v Christou* (10) the House of Lords confirmed that the question of severing the counts on sexual offences which are similar to each other, but where the evidence is not cross-admissible between the different offences, so as to ensure separate trials, is purely one for the discretion of the trial judge. If he decides not to sever, he must (simply!) ensure that the jury understand the position on the significance of the evidence on each count and keep the matters separate.

It seems as if the cumulative effect of *R v P, R v H* and *R v Christou* is such that, in other than identification situations, most of the safeguards of the last hundred years or so have been jettisoned and the position for the person standing accused of the most mundane types of offence, possibly even in situations where witness collusion is a possibility, will be one of enormous difficulty in keeping out evidence having overwhelming potential for prejudice.

The conclusion to be drawn seems to be that either the earlier courts were right about the dangers of this evidence or the modern judges are right about its relative safety. Both cannot be right. It may be said that the effect of recent similar fact cases has clarified the law by distinguishing between cases where identification is in issue (where something akin to a 'signature' must be present to justify the admissibility) and non-identification cases where much less will suffice. It may also be said that leaving collusion to a jury may have simplified matters. Whether a jury in such a situation would find the law clearer is greatly to be doubted; time alone will tell.

References

(1) [1894] AC 57
(2) [1952] AC 694
(3) [1975] AC 421
(4) (1977) 67 Cr App R 143
(5) (1976) 65 Cr App R 107
(6) [1991] 3 All ER 337
(7) [1992] Crim LR 428
(8) *Current Law*, November 1997, 129
(9) [1995] 2 All ER 865
(10) [1996] 2 All ER 927

QUESTION 4

'It is the principle behind the right to silence, not its practical effect, which makes it necessary to reverse the recent reforms.'
　Discuss.

SUGGESTED SOLUTION TO QUESTION 4

General Comment

This question gives a considerable latitude to the candidate in deciding the form and shape of answer, but there is a proposition here that must be supported or rebutted. Any answer that fails to do either is likely to receive low marks. It will be necessary to discuss the scope and rationale for the so-called right of silence as well as the arguments and process that led to the erosion of the rights. The legislative changes and the guidance given by the case law should be looked at if a complete view of the defendant's situation is to be achieved. By way of conclusion, a firm view, supported by reasoning, should be taken of the proposition.

Skeleton Solution

The defendant's right to silence; extent of the right and legal rationale.

The evidential effects of silence.

The pressure for change and the legislative changes.

Case-law development.

Conclusion.

Suggested Solution

The so-called 'right to silence' of an accused person consists of various identifiable options open to him, ranging from matters occurring before he is even a suspect right up to the events occurring during his trial. A person may quite properly refuse to answer to police at all stages from initial questioning right through to interviews under detention conditions. He may properly refuse to give evidence or, having been sworn, to answer particular questions and be free from compulsion on the matter. A person had, until recently, the right that his failure to give evidence or to answer questions should not have the consequence of permitting prosecution comment or jury inferences adverse to his position. These rights were, until recent changes, subject only to minor legislative inroads and they have their origins in the reaction to the legally permissible compulsion of accused persons formerly associated with prerogative powers and institutions, such as the Star Chamber Court. Since the Civil War swept away such compulsion, the common law and statute (s1(a), (b) Criminal Evidence Act 1898) has largely seen these rights as inviolate both as to freedom from compulsion as well as from adverse effects.

Quite a different matter is the evidential effect of silence and an understanding of this is necessary for a proper perspective on silence. There is ample authority for the proposition that, as between persons who are speaking 'on even terms', a reaction of silence in the face of an accusation which would normally call for some answer is capable of constituting evidence that the accused acknowledged the truth of the accusation: *R v Mitchell* (1); *R v Norton* (2); *R v Chandler* (3). Such a silence, equating to acceptance, is admissible along with the accusation because the silence equates to a confession by conduct within s82(1) Police and Criminal Evidence Act (PACE) 1984 and to an informal admission at common law. The matter changes rapidly, however, once the accused and accuser cease to be speaking 'on even terms'. According to Lord Diplock in *Hall v R* (4), silence cannot give rise to an inference of acceptance in the latter situation, usually where the police are questioning a person as a suspect. Nevertheless, there are many cases where *Hall* has been distinguished and an accused taken to have been on even terms with the accuser (usually the victim) despite the presence of the police as in *R v Horne* (5) and also in *Chandler*. The trend has been away from *Hall* in recent years.

Despite the fundamental nature of the rights involved in silence, very great public dissatisfaction arose at the ease with which many defendants appeared able to evade justice by resorting to silence in the knowledge that this could do their case no harm and might well allow their very silence, as a right, to inject reasonable doubt into the trial. There was also great unease at the idea of defendants being permitted to advance defences and matters at trial for the first time, long after any satisfactory investigations into the matter had ceased to be possible. A Royal Commission under Lord Runciman in 1993 recommended that no inferences should be drawn based on silence under police questioning, but the experience of Northern Ireland legislation, based on recommendations of the Criminal Law Revision Committee, showed that there was a supportable case for allowing inferences to be drawn from silence. Parliament took the initiative in ss34–39 Criminal Justice and Public Order Act (CJPOA) 1994. Experience with Northern Ireland legislation had also paved the way for allowing adverse comment by the prosecution and adverse inferences to be drawn from failure to give evidence. The effects of ss34–39 CJPOA 1994 allow for proper inferences and comment upon failure to mention facts when questioned under caution or when charged (s34), upon a defendant of 14 years or older declining to give evidence or, once sworn, refusing to answer a question without good cause (s35), failing to account for marks, substances etc after arrest (s36), and failure to account for his presence at the time and place of arrest (s37).

The massive changes have been developed and complemented by case-law development such as the possibility that remaining silent on the advice of a legal advisor will not, of itself, be 'good cause' for the purposes of s34: *R v Condron* (6). *R v Cowan* (7) has provided the Court of Appeal guidelines on the drawing of appropriate inferences under s35 and the width of the judicial discretion whether to direct or not against drawing inferences seems very considerable. The judge does not have so much discretion as to the matters that he must direct the jury about but, undoubtly, a much greater responsibility falls upon the judge since these changes.

It would be folly to pretend that the legal right to silence has not been greatly reduced and weakened by the cumulative effect of these changes, but it should be also remembered that the evidential effect of silence has long shown the risks attendant on maintaining silence where some answer might be expected. No compulsion has crept in here at all. There are no echoes of the Court of Star Chamber; all that has happened is the recognition of drawing logical inferences where it is proper to do so and, even then, no conviction can follow on the inferences alone: s38(3) CJPOA 1994. The principle underlying the right to silence never was based as much on a privilege against self-incrimination as on a protection against compulsion of accused persons. This principle is unaffected by the changes and it is submitted that there are no good arguments for reversing the reforms. The notion that there is a right to silence should not, in today's enlightened climate with a comprehensive evidence code under PACE 1984, carry with it a certain consequence that remaining silent should have no adverse effect whatever for an accused. This would be totally illogical.

References

(1)   (1892) 17 Co CC 503
(2)   [1910] 2 KB 496
(3)   [1976] 1 WLR 585
(4)   [1971] 1 All ER 322
(5)   [1990] Crim LR 188
(6)   [1997] 1 Cr App R 185
(7)   [1995] 4 All ER 939

QUESTION 5

Andrew is charged with murdering Brian. The prosecution claimed that Andrew knifed Brian outside his house because he thought that Brian was having an affair with Carol, Andrew's wife. Andrew claims that he was defending himself because Brian attacked him when Andrew told him to 'put a stop to this nonsense with Carol'. A month before he died, Brian e-mailed his brother, saying he was scared because Andrew had found out about Carol and that he, Brian, would be 'looking over his shoulder from now on'. Doreen, Brian's sister, was staying at Brian's on the night of the stabbing. She has stated to the police that she heard angry voices, amongst them Brian's voice, outside the house at the time. When the noise subsided, she went out to check and found Brian lying on the ground, bleeding, with no-one around. Brian said 'I tried to fend him off. He just went crazy.' Doreen says she won't testify because of anonymous telephone calls warning her against doing so. Sid, a detective who was pretending to be a prisoner at the time Andrew was in custody, says that he drew Andrew into a conversation in which Andrew said 'I gave Brian a right hiding. He had it coming to him all along.'

Discuss any evidential issues arising.

SUGGESTED SOLUTION TO QUESTION 5

General Comment

With such a situation, structuring an answer is important and one technique which suggests itself here is to deal with prosecution and defence evidence separately. Much of the question deals with the hearsay rule, but it is important to deal with other points, such as the burdens on Andrew's defence, compellability of witnesses, s23 Criminal Justice Act 1988 and ss76 and 78 Police and Criminal Evidence Act (PACE) 1984.

Skeleton Solution

a) Brian's defence evidence; the burdens involved.

Proof that Brian was aware that Andrew knew about the affair; the e-mail, was it printed or stored?; the hearsay rule, showing state of mind.

Proof of the angry voices by Doreen; Doreen's unwillingness to testify; hearsay evidence.

b) The prosecution evidence.

Proof of Brian's e-mail to show Brian's fear of Andrew.

Doreen's evidence: the statement; multiple hearsay; the exceptions for spontaneous utterances; *Andrews*; non-hearsay statements; *Ratten*.

Andrew's confession; ss76, 78 PACE; breaches of Code C.

Suggested Solution

a) *Andrew's defence evidence*

Andrew is relying on self-defence and will have to discharge the evidential burden upon this matter which will be almost impossible unless he gives evidence, leaving the legal burden to rebut it upon the prosecution. An important element of his defence is that Brian was aware that Andrew knew of his wife's affair; it supports Andrew's story of a 'warning-off' approach rather than a murderous ambush. Andrew might wish to make use of the e-mail to the brother for this purpose. Brian's words are conceptually hearsay if reproduced in court for their truth, so this problem must be overcome. If the e-mail had been printed off, or was still stored on computer disc or drive, this would constitute a document within the definition applicable to criminal evidence under the Criminal Justice Act (CJA) 1988. As a first-hand hearsay document, this would be prima facie admissible under s23 CJA 1988 as meeting the requirement in s23(2)(a) of the maker being dead, but it would be subject to the exclusionary discretion in s25.

If the e-mail was not recorded or printed anywhere there would be no possibility of using s23, and the matter would have to be oral hearsay via the testimony of the brother. This would probably be admissible under the common law hearsay exception of res gestae statements showing the state of mind of the speaker as in *Neill v North Antrim Magistrates' Court* (1).

Andrew will almost certainly wish to get into court Doreen's evidence to the effect that she heard angry words. This is consistent with his story and he may get the advantage of this if Doreen gives prosecution evidence or her statement is allowed in by the judge (see below). If the prosecution do not use her evidence, Andrew may decide to call her and he could compel her. If she refused to give evidence, once sworn upon the point, he could possibly apply to the judge to treat her as hostile following *R v Thompson* (2) and to put her earlier statement to her under s3 Criminal Procedure Act 1865. The prosecution might object to her evidence of angry words on the ground that there is a hearsay implication. This could be met with the argument, used by the Privy Council in *Ratten v R* (3), that the evidence is non-hearsay evidence of 'the state of affairs' obtaining at a particular time and place, which is the issue here.

b) *The prosecution evidence*

It sounds likely that the prosecution will wish to put Brian's e-mail into evidence to show that he was already in fear of Brian. As outlined in para a) above, there should not be too many difficulties getting this in under s23 CJA 1988 if in a document, or under the common law exception if it is oral. The common law exception might be used if the court wished to exclude it in the exercise of its discretion under s23 if it was recorded. The fact that the statutory route was not open would not, of itself, bar a common law exception.

As to Doreen's evidence, the prosecution will surely wish to get Brian's last words into evidence. The defence will wish to keep them out as being inconsistent with Andrew's evidence and will try to use the hearsay rule. It should be possible to argue that this matter falls within the exception for res gestae spontaneous utterances made whilst the speaker's mind is dominated by some shocking or startling event. The leading case on this now is *R v Andrews* (4), and Brian seems to have been well within the state of domination of thoughts outlined by Lord Ackner. There is still the very real problem that Doreen will not testify because of fear. There has been a growing use of s23(3)(b) CJA 1988 in recent times, as in *R v Acton JJ, ex parte McMullen* (5) to admit witness statements made to the police, but there are two problems here. One is the necessity for leave under the inclusionary discretion in s26 CJA 1988 for a police investigation document, and the second is the question whether, as this is repetition of a hearsay statement via an exception, this is 'direct oral evidence by' Doreen or is it second-hand hearsay. If it is the latter, s23 will not help. The use of 'direct' seems to indicate that s23 will not help. If, by contrast, Brian's words can be seen as indicative of a state of affairs which is in issue, *Ratten v R* is authority that this is not hearsay at all and Doreen could give 'direct' evidence of it and, consequently, her documentary evidence would fit within s23. A further possibility might be available under s24 CJA 1988.

Andrew has been tricked into making a confession at a time when he was in custody and within the protections of Code C of PACE 1984. The question here is first, whether the confession is admissible in law and, second, whether, if it is, it can be excluded as a matter of discretion. The first point is dealt with by reference to s76 PACE 1984 which shows that it will be inadmissible if shown to be obtained by oppression (s76(2)(a)) or by reason of things said or done which were likely in the circumstances to render any confession by him unreliable: s76(2)(b). It sounds very unlikely that the trickery could amount to oppression within the extended meaning of that term shown in *R v Fulling* (6). Trickery that does not sap the will of the doctrine is not usually sufficient: *R v Parker* (7). Again, with s76(2)(b), there seems nothing tending towards unreliability so probably the confession is admissible in law.

As regards exclusion by discretion, s78 PACE will allow for exclusion on the basis of the adverse effects on the fairness of the proceedings. The police action drives a coach and horses through the provisions of Code C for the questioning of suspects. This is the classic example of the 'significant and substantial' breaches of the 'verballing' provisions so disliked by the Court of Appeal in *R v Keenan* (8). Such a deliberate and flagrant disregard of the Code and the worst of bad faith is almost certain to lead to the confession being excluded under s78.

References

(1) [1992] 4 All ER 846
(2) (1976) 64 Cr App R 96
(3) [1972] AC 378
(4) [1987] 1 All ER 513
(5) (1991) 92 Cr App R 98
(6) (1987) 85 Cr App R 136
(7) [1995] Cr LR 233
(8) [1989] 3 All ER 598

QUESTION 6

After a knife fight at a club, the police question everyone present. After this, and as a result, Ewan, Fred and George are arrested and charged with wounding with intent. During this initial questioning, Ewan makes a couple of admissions. The police search him at the police station, before his solicitor arrives, and they find that he has a number of pills. The police ask him what these are, and Ewan admits that they are 'a controlled drug'. Fred barely speaks English. The police hold him for nine hours while they obtain an interpreter. They then interview him and, in due course, he admits that he was involved in the fight. As a result of what Fred says, a bloody knife is found in a garden next door to the club. George is of very low intelligence, but the police are not aware of this, and George looks up to Ewan and Fred as his superiors. The police tell George that Ewan and Fred have admitted to being in the fight and, on hearing this, George admits that he himself took part and, further, played the major role. All three were offered access to a solicitor as soon as they reached the station, but only Ewan accepted the offer.

Discuss any evidential issues arising.

SUGGESTED SOLUTION TO QUESTION 6

General Comment
Students attempting this type of question should be prepared to show some knowledge of Code C PACE 1984 and the problems attached to evidence obtained by the police directly from the accused. A detailed knowledge of confessions and ss76 and 78 is called for, as well as a good answer structure showing the interrelationship of the various items of evidence but, at the same time, keeping the evidential points on each accused separate.

Skeleton Solution

Ewan
The admissions made under initial question.
Were cautions required?
The search, the pills and Ewan's answer.

Fred
The reason for his arrest.
The delay and use of interpreter.
His confession.
The offer of legal advice.
The evidential use of the knife: s76(4)(5).

George
Sections 76 and 77.
The means of obtaining the confession: s78.
The offer of access to legal advice.
The interrelationship of the evidence.

Suggested Solution

Ewan
Ewan has made some admissions during initial questioning, presumably without caution. Generally a statement wholly or partly adverse to him will be within the Police and Criminal Evidence Act (PACE) 1984 definition of a confession (s82(1)) and be admissible against him subject to s76 PACE 1984. It sounds likely that 'initial questioning' would not imply oppression within s76(2)(a), and there are no indications that the admissions were obtained in

consequence of things 'said or done' tending towards unreliability of the statements: s76(2)(b). As a matter of law, the confessions are likely to be admissible. A point that should be considered is whether, after a serious crime in a (perhaps small) club with, perhaps, few persons present, everyone present might be considered a suspect so that questioning only takes place under caution. Section 10.1 of Code C states a person whom there are grounds to suspect of an offence must be cautioned before questioning if his answers are to be given in evidence. This is a basic and fundamentally important right of a suspect, and failure to give a caution at the appropriate time is a justification for the discretionary exclusion of the answers to police questions: *R v Hunt* (1).

The police search Ewan after the arrest, find pills and get what might be damaging admission. Ewan should have been cautioned under section 10.3 Code C but, assuming that he was, this fresh turn of events may well constitute an 'interview' within section 11.1A about a completely different offence and, again, a fresh caution should be given before questioning (section 11.2A). Thus, as before, there may be a problem in using his answer against him. There is no requirement under Part 4 of Code C for the solicitor to be present during this search which seems to be authorised within section 4.1. The only problem with using Ewan's answer about the drug against him may be the lack of proper cautioning and the s78 discretion.

Fred
As Fred barely speaks English, it begs the question as to why he was arrested in the first place. What reasonable grounds of suspicion were there? Evidence in the form of a confession obtained as a result of wrongful arrest would be likely to fall within s76(2)(a) as obtained by oppression and thus be inadmissible in law regardless of the truth of the confession. The offer of legal advice on arriving at the station would be of no use to Fred as he would be unlikely to have understood it. Unless the offer were repeated through an interpreter, Fred has been denied another of his most fundamental rights, that of legal advice, under s58 PACE 1984 and Part 6 of Code C. This confession is almost certain to fall foul of both limbs of s76(2), as well as the discretion to exclude under s78: *R v Samuel* (2).

The delay in obtaining an interpreter would not be significant, provided that his conditions of detention fell reasonably within Part 8 of Code C and the use of the interpreter seems to show the police attempting compliance with Part 13 of the Code. The real problem is that the confession by Fred is almost certain to be excluded as explained above. Nevertheless, his confession has led to the discovery of the knife. This knife has two evidential aspects. The first is that it may carry upon it traces of its user – blood, prints etc – or of its provenance, ie the evidence of someone who recalled selling this particular knife to someone. There would be no problems about this because the mere fact that it was found as the result of an inadmissible confession would not render it inadmissible as evidence: s76(4)(a) PACE 1984. The second aspect would be to show that it was found as the result of a confession by Fred, ie linking him to it. This is completely impermissible except by Fred's own evidence: s76(5).

George
George has made a confession after hearing that the other two have confessed. There are several problems about this. The first is that if George is mentally handicapped, his understanding of the need for a solicitor would be defective. He would have needed to be interviewed in the presence of an 'independent person' or 'appropriate adult' and, if not, a special warning will have to be given to the jury under s77 PACE 1984: Annex C, Code C. The police handling of this matter is probably well within 'oppression' for the purposes of s76. Even if not inadmissible by s76, it is almost certain to fall foul of s78: *R v Silcott* (3).

The offer of access to legal advice to the three suspects at the arrival at the station would, effectively, only have been offered to Ewan. The other pair were simply, rather cynically, denied the right. This will, almost by itself, deny their evidence to the prosecution.

The interrelationship between the evidence is that the confessions, where admissible, are evidence only against their maker, not against the others: *Lobban v R* (4). The only applicable exception to that principle is if there is a common design or conspiracy involved in the offence(s). Here the confessions, if relating to acts in the furtherance of the conspiracy, are admissible against other members: *R v Blake and Tye* (5). The knife, of course, may be evidence against any of them.

References

(1)   [1992] Crim LR 582
(2)   [1988] 2 All ER 135
(3)   [1987] Crim LR 765
(4)   [1995] 2 All ER 602
(5)   (1844) 6 QB 126

QUESTION 7

Half-Life Radiation plc, is collaborating with the Chemistry department of Faustus University. Together they are developing methods of producing chemical and radiated rain clouds for use by the Ministry of Defence. Particularly under investigation is the possibility of irradiating water with the use of small pellets of uranium. Harold, a lecturer in philosophy, who is investigating the moral status of such work, receives a massive overdose of radiation when he finds a batch of these pellets which have been carelessly left unprotected. He brings a negligence action against Half-Life Radiation plc, but the defendants refuse to disclose a report made by a special committee consisting of members of the Law and Chemistry departments of Faustus University. This committee had been created by the university after there had been a radiation leakage some years earlier. The terms of the Committee were 'to investigate the causes of accidents at Faustus'. Harold persuades his sister, Irene, who works for Half-Life Radiation plc, to give him a computer file of this report for him, saying that he needs it for his research. This file is clearly marked 'Confidential'. Harold finds that it contains summaries of statements made by staff involved in the accident and the conclusions of the committee. Harold seeks to have this document admitted in evidence.

Advise Half-Life Radiation plc.

SUGGESTED SOLUTION TO QUESTION 7

General Comment

The question requires an overview of the various types of privilege and immunity that can attach to sensitive communications and of how, and by whom, the protections can be invoked. The aspects of the report connected with hearsay and computer recording, as well as its opinion nature, should be dealt with. The use of secondary evidence should be discussed.

Skeleton Solution

The legal protections suggested by the question and the persons who could invoke them:

a) Legal professional privilege and the University/Half-Life Radiation plc.

b) The privilege against self-incrimination and the University/Half-Life Radiation plc.

c) Public interest immunity: Half-Life Radiation plc, the University, the Ministry of Defence and the court.

d) Confidentiality and Irene.

Secondary evidence: the rule in *Calcraft* v *Guest*, injunction.

The hearsay and opinion aspects of the evidence.

Civil Evidence Act 1995, discovery and notice, computer evidence.

Suggested Solution

The evidence of the copy report raises several possibilities of privilege and immunity of such evidence which might give the opportunity to the various persons in the question to object to the use of the report in evidence and its consequent publication. It is assumed that Half-Life plc and the University are partners in joint enterprise:

a) *Half-Life Radiation plc/the University and legal professional privilege*

The fact that the special committee consists in part of lawyers suggests that providing a legal advice component might be a normal part of its remit despite the narrow nature of its terms of undertaking. Communications between lawyer and client for the purpose of giving and receiving legal advice are protected, in the hands of the lawyer and client, by legal professional privilege. This will extend to in-house lawyers: *Alfred Crompton Amusement Machines Ltd* v *Customs and Excise Commissioners (No 2)* (1). This would be likely to cover any views of the lawyers in the report. The privilege also extends to communications with third parties (such as the scientists on the committee) where the dominant purpose of the communication is actual or contemplated litigation: *Waugh v British Railways Board* (2). It is a question of fact whether this is the dominant purpose here but, even if it is not, the protected part of the report may well prevent disclosure of the whole unless some severance is properly available: *Re Sarah C Getty Trust* (3). Half-Life and the University could invoke this privilege for themselves and against the committee members; the question against others is discussed below.

b) *Half-Life Radiation plc/the University and the privilege against self-incrimination*
There is a long-established principle that no-one is bound to answer questions if, in the opinion of the judge, to do so would expose him to criminal charge or penalty: *Blunt v Park Lane Hotels* (4). Although rather disapproved of in the civil context by the House of Lords in *AT & T Instel v Tully* (5), exposure to prosecution under the health and safety at work or nuclear radiation legislation would allow the University to argue against producing or answering questions about the report, but would probably not be enough to justify injunctions against its use. The other problem with this is that the University cannot refuse to answer problems which incriminate its staff and vice versa. The privilege is only against self-incrimination: *Tate Access Floors v Boswell* (6).

c) *Public interest immunity: Half-Life Radiation plc, the University, the Ministry of Defence and the court*
There is a very wide range of matters where evidence may be withheld from disclosure on the basis that to do so would harm various public interests to an extent sufficient to outweigh the public interest in the administration of justice. Interests of national defence carry very great weight in this regard (*Duncan v Cammell Laird and Co Ltd* (7)), but the courts, since the House of Lords judgments in *Conway v Rimmer* (8), have taken the view that very few documents are of such a class of importance as to be beyond, at least, scrutiny by the judges to see whether the claim to non-disclosure is justified on public interest grounds. It does seem to be the case that public interest immunity certificates signed by ministers of the Crown are fairly conclusive of the question where matters of national security are concerned: *Balfour v Foreign and Commonwealth Office* (9). This privilege could be invoked by any person in possession of the report and should be taken by the judge at his own instance if others fail to do so: *Duncan v Cammell Laird and Co Ltd*.

d) *Irene and the 'confidential' file*
Confidentiality is not by itself a sufficient ground to protect material against disclosure but it is still a very important matter. Section 10 Contempt of Court Act 1981 shows that national security is sufficient to outweigh confidentiality of sources. In our situation confidentiality, national security and public interest all go hand in hand to keep this report from disclosure

at the instance of Irene or anyone else in the question. The one person who could not keep it from disclosure, if he wished to do so, would be Harold himself where disclosure was sought to identify the source of the leak: *Secretary of State for Defence* v *Guardian Newspapers Ltd* (10).

The mere fact that legal professional privilege covered the report would not prevent the use of secondary evidence in the hands of another (*Calcraft* v *Guest* (11)) but, as a general rule, injunctions and orders for delivering up of the file would usually be available to the owner of the privilege, the University: *Lord Ashburton* v *Pape* (12).

Even if there were no difficulties with privilege or immunity, questions might be raised about the hearsay rule and the opinion aspects of the report (assuming that there are opinions expressed). The fact that these are opinions of experts as distinct from laypersons would tend towards their admissibility about issues requiring the need for such expertise: *Folkes* v *Chadd* (13). The hearsay problem is removed, as a question of admissibility by s1(1) Civil Evidence Act (CEA) 1995, but the main problem is that compliance must be made with RSC O.38 r36 requiring the court to consider the question of disclosure, thus preventing any ambush by Harold. The inevitable result of all of this is that all questions of the admissibility of the report and its privileged or immune status are likely to need resolution at an interlocutory stage. One question which has now been much simplified by s13 CEA 1995 is the assimilation of the treatment of computer-stored or -generated documents to that of any other documents compared to the earlier cumbersome treatment of computer documents by s5 Civil Evidence Act 1968. No special problems will attach to the report because of its computer-stored quality.

References

(1) [1974] AC 405
(2) [1980] AC 521
(3) [1985] QB 956
(4) [1942] 2 KB 253
(5) [1992] 3 All ER 523
(6) [1990] 3 All ER 303
(7) [1942] AC 624
(8) [1968] AC 910
(9) [1994] 2 All ER 588
(10) [1984] 3 All ER 601
(11) [1898] 1 QB 759
(12) [1913] 2 Ch 469
(13) (1782) 3 Doug KB 157

QUESTION 8

Joe and Kevin are charged with burglary of Lolita's house and Mervin is charged with handling a gold bracelet stolen in the burglary. Lolita testifies at trial that two men entered her bedroom one night. One, whom she identifies as Joe, held her down while the other, who was wearing a stocking over his face, ransacked her drawers. When they had gone, she called the police. Noel, a police officer, testifies that while driving to Lolita's house, he gave chase to two men who had acted suspiciously on seeing the police car. He stopped one, who was Kevin. Kevin had a stocking in his hand, and admitted the burglary. Noel also testifies that he found Lolita's bracelet when he later went to Mervin's jewellery shop. Joe testifies that on the night of the burglary he was in another town, attending Alcoholics Anonymous. He says he has 'never seen Mervin in his life'. Joe has two convictions, one for a bank robbery and another for taking ruby rings in a burglary. Kevin testifies that he tried to evade Noel because he'd 'had cops on him before'. Kevin says that when he was arrested he said [he] 'hadn't done anything', when accused of burglary. Kevin has been convicted for indecent assaults on young children and for tax evasion. Mervin testifies that he bought the bracelet from Joe, who had told him he was selling for his wife. In fact, Mervin had already told the police that he'd bought the bracelet from a 'man in the street'. Mervin's interview with the police is excluded by the trial judge because it contravened the Code of Practice.

Discuss the cross-examination of Joe, Kevin and Mervin.

QUESTION 8 SOLUTION TO QUESTION 8

Joe and Kevin are charged with burglary of Lolita's house and Mervin is charged with handling a gold bracelet stolen in the burglary. Lolita testifies at trial that two men entered her bedroom one night, that one of them, whom she later identifies as Joe, laid her down while the other, who was, presumably, about to rape her, but first ransacked her drawers. When the first thing she called the police. When a police officer testifies that while driving to Lolita's house he gave chase to two men who had acted suspiciously on seeing the police car. He stopped one, who was Kevin. Kevin had a stocking in his hand, and admitted the burglary. Noel also testifies that he found Lolita's bracelet when he later went to Mervin's jewellery shop. Joe testifies that on the night of the burglary he was in another town attending Alcoholics Anonymous. He says he has never seen Mervin in his life. Joe has two convictions, one for a bank robbery and another for taking ruby rings in a burglary. Kevin testifies that he tried to evade Noel because he had cops on him before. Kevin says that when he was arrested he said that he hadn't done anything. When accused of burglary, Kevin has been convicted for indecent assault on young children and for tax evasion. Mervin testifies that he bought the bracelet from Joe, who had told him he was selling for his wife. In fact, Mervin had already told the police that he bought the bracelet from a man in the street. Mervin's interview with the police is excluded by the trial judge because it contravened the Code of Practice.

Discuss the cross-examination of Joe, Kevin and Mervin.

SUGGESTED SOLUTION TO QUESTION 8

General Comment

A fairly complex interplay of the rules on cross-examination, the question calls for careful planning if clarity is to be achieved. One approach is to take each witness separately, list the matters upon which they could be cross-examined and deal with any rules governing each evidential point as it arises. Remember that cross-examination can extend to matters in issue even though not dealt with in-chief as well as to credit.

Skeleton Solution

Joe

Matters raised by his evidence: the alibi; his statement about Mervin; the collateral evidence rule.

Other matters: matters arising from Lolita's evidence; Mervin's evidence about Joe; his convictions; s1(f) Criminal Evidence Act 1898; Joe's evidence 'against' Mervin.

Kevin

Matters raised by his evidence; his suspicious actions; trouble with the police; s1(f) Criminal Evidence Act 1898; *Jones* v *DPP*.

Other matters: matters arising from Noel's evidence; matters arising from Lolita's evidence; his convictions; s1(f) Criminal Evidence Act 1898; his earlier confession.

Mervin

Matters raised by his evidence; his evidence 'against' Joe; s1(f)(iii) Criminal Evidence Act 1898; cross-examination by Joe and by the prosecution.

Other matters: matters arising from Noel's evidence; Mervin's earlier inconsistent statement to the police.

Possible assertion of good character by Mervin; s1(f)(ii) Criminal Evidence Act 1898.

Suggested Solution

Joe

The prosecution may wish to cross examine Joe about various matters raised by his examination in chief. They may quite properly ask him about any facts in issue, of which one will be his alibi, to seek to strengthen the prosecution case

53

or to weaken the defence evidence. They will also be permitted to ask questions about his acquaintance with Mervin as being in issue. The prosecution may also, within limits ask questions about Joe's credibility within the limits set out in *Hobbs* v *Tinling* (1) and *R* v *Sweet Escott* (2). The questioning on credit will also be limited (by the rule of finality of answers to collateral questions) to exceptional matters as set out in *Attorney-General* v *Hitchcock* (3).

Joe may be asked about other matters such as arise from Lolita's or Mervin's evidence. He might properly be asked about the events in Lolita's bedroom and the circumstances of her identification; also about Mervin's version of Joe's participation. Mervin would have been able to repeat Joe's explanation, despite its hearsay nature, on the basis of it being a 'confession' within s82(1) Police and Criminal Evidence Act (PACE) 1984. There is nothing 'collateral' about these matters and, similarly, he could be asked about matters raised by Noel's evidence. Clearly, prolonged questioning about these matters runs the risk of becoming collateral or even irrelevant if it goes too far.

The prosecution may also wish to ask questions about Joe's previous convictions. The questioning will be governed by s1(f) Criminal Evidence Act (CEA) 1898. This will only permit questioning if the offences were relevant to prove the instant charge within the similar fact doctrine (s1(f)(i)), which seems doubtful here, or if Joe has lost his shield under s1(f)(ii) or (iii). There are no indications that Joe has crossed the line on either of the two situations set out in s1(f)(ii). If he had, the questioning would have been governed by the guidelines set out by the Court of Appeal in *R* v *McLeod* (4). The primary purpose of this questioning is as to credibility and the jury must be told this, but this will not necessarily prevent questioning about offences similar to that charged as in *R* v *Powell* (5). Joe might, however, have 'given evidence against' Mervin by undermining his defence: *Murdoch* v *Taylor* (6). This would cause loss of shield under s1(f)(iii) against cross-examination by counsel for Mervin and, by leave of the judge, the prosecution. Again the questioning goes to credibility: *Murdoch* v *Taylor*.

Kevin
Similarly, Kevin may be properly cross-examined about issues raised by his own evidence, and about the confession made upon being detained by Noel, subject to there being no ss76 or 78 PACE 1984 problems attaching to it. This will probably have been already introduced into evidence by Noel under s76 and Kevin may be asked about it, despite the collateral evidence rule, as a previous inconsistent oral statement within the requirements of s4 Criminal Procedure Act 1865. This would not, in any case, be a collateral issue, but instead, clearly 'relative to the subject matter of the indictment' within s4.

Kevin's evidence of having been in trouble with the police has probably removed his protection under s1(f)(ii) or (iii) under the view taken by the House of Lords in *Jones* v *DPP* (7), whereby any loss of shield is caused by the accused revealing his own convictions. Even if this were not the case, Kevin is clearly making an imputation that Noel has fabricated his confession; no other view can be taken of the matter following *R v Britzman, R v Hall* (8), so the shield would inevitably be lost. The questioning, as before, would be about credit and be governed by *R v McLeod*. Kevin could properly be asked about any matter raised by Noel's evidence of suspicious actions and the stocking or about Lolita's evidence concerning the stocking and, presumably, about the stocking itself.

Mervin
Mervin can be crossed-examined about his own evidence by the prosecution. He has also very clearly 'given evidence against' Joe within s1(f)(iii), both strengthening the prosecution case and weakening Joe's defence within the guidelines in *Murdoch v Taylor*, and this would cost him his shield against examination on the discreditable matters set out in s1(f) by counsel for Joe, or, with leave of the judge, by the prosecution. We are not told of anything particularly discreditable in Mervin's past but Joe's counsel will need to ask, if he can, about Mervin's earlier excluded statement. This does not need any shield to be lost because an accused may, as of right, examine a co-accused about an inadmissible confession which is relevant to the defence of the accused, provided that the judge directs the jury that the statement is not to be used as evidence of its maker's guilt: *R v Rowson* (9). This right applies only to cross-examination on behalf of an accused not the prosecution.

It is very unlikely that the judge, having excluded the earlier statement as inadmissible, would now allow prosecution cross-examination about it simply to attack credibility. The Court of Appeal in *R v Treacy* (10) held this to be completely impermissible. Mervin could properly be examined about matters arising from Noel's evidence other than the earlier statement.

It sounds possible here that Mervin (if he has no convictions) might be tempted to put his good character into evidence to get the advantage of a *R v Vye* (11) direction. The prosecution would be able to cross-examine on this because of a loss of shield under s1(f)(ii) as could counsel for Joe, presumably by leave of the judge; possibly even counsel for Kevin, again, by leave.

References

(1) [1929] 2 KB 1
(2) (1971) 55 Cr App R 316
(3) (1847) 1 Exch 91
(4) [1994] 3 All ER 254
(5) [1985] 1 All ER 193
(6) [1965] AC 574
(7) [1962] AC 635
(8) [1983] 1 WLR 350
(9) [1985] 2 All ER 539
(10) [1944] 2 All ER 229
(11) [1993] 1 WLR 471